To my wife, who makes life so, very fun.

Dysfunctional Leadership
A Few Easy Steps to Generate Chaos in the Workplace

This book is prompted by some of my own personal experiences. As with anything, my perspective may be skewed by my own bias. However, perspective is important. If my perspective, as an employee, is that of dysfunction, then the dysfunction exists. If many employees believe there is a dysfunction, then there is a problem in the organization that should be addressed. I am not saying that the employees are always correct, but there is a problem that must be addressed when several employees believe there is a dysfunctionality in the workplace. The leader or manager has a responsibility to fix whatever is wrong with the culture or environment and correct whatever may be causing angst amongst the employees.

For background on my mindset as I pen this book, I believe the boss deserves all the respect and privilege of his position. The boss has certain tasks and responsibilities that are his to accomplish. Similarly, my tasks as an employee and subordinate are mine to accomplish. If I fail, the failures are mine...not that of the organization or my supervisor. Additionally, my agreements with the organization are mine alone and have no bearing on another employee. If another employee is paid twice as much for the same work, I really don't care...his agreement with the company is different than mine and is none of my concern. With this in mind, if a manager or supervisor does something to foment a caustic or toxic environment, I take note of it. However, I also realize that nobody is perfect. Many times the weight of leadership positions can cause people to do unusual things. Some people are simply insecure about their leadership, so they act in a manner that is caustic to the work environment. Sometimes well-meaning people can do some pretty harmful things. Over my 30+ years of working, I have seen many examples of poor leadership. This book is a snapshot of some of my observations.

If you find yourself as a subject in this book, it is OK. Many of us have found ourselves, at one time or another, in the midst of being the boss that we hoped we would not be. We all have potential to display the adverse characteristics found in the coming chapters. All of us fall short at times and must constantly assess ourselves and find those areas in which we can improve.

Preface to the November 2020 Update

If you are reading this paragraph, you have the November 2020 version of this book. The update was inspired by a discussion with a friend who noted an odd behavior by his boss. The dysfunction we discussed formed the basis for chapter 12.

Preface to the June 2021 Update

No new dysfunctions are included, but the text has been updated for clarity of thought.

Preface to the August 2022 Update

A new chapter has been added as chapter 13. The data comes from an experience with a large corporation that was successful on paper, but a miserable place to work. The company did some things right, but many things wrong, resulting in high turnover and very poor employee reviews.

Table of Contents

Chapter 1: The Rogue Manager...Eager, but Inane
....6

Chapter 2: The Leader Who Loves to Make Decisions..9

Chapter 3: The Checklist Leader Who Only Cares About Himself...12

Chapter 4: The Disappointing Jerk......................15

Chapter 5: The Boss that Cannot Speak Clearly..17

Chapter 6: The Bully 19

Chapter 7: The Energetic Idiot...........................20

Chapter 8: The Paralyzed Leader 21

Chapter 9: The Leader Who Loves Himself.........22

Chapter 10: The Leader Who Loves Meetings....23

Chapter 11: Too Busy with His Personal Life 24

Chapter 12: Keeping Secrets.............................25

Chapter 13: The Ungrateful Leader 26

Chapter 14: Conclusion.....................................29

Chapter 1: The Rogue Manager...Eager, but Inane

Scenario 1: A construction corporation builds low-budget homes and has a construction department and warranty department. The construction department builds homes and is responsible for maintenance and repairs of the home until it is purchased by the customer. he construction department is required to correct any deficiencies identified during the construction period. Before the buyer purchases the home, the warranty department conducts a quality check on the home and the construction department must correct any issues discovered by that quality check. After the buyer purchases the home, the warranty department is responsible for correcting any newly identified deficiencies and the construction department no longer has any jurisdiction over the home.

The above process existed and worked flawlessly for several months. Out of the blue, the warranty manager, without consulting anyone, decided it wasn't a good idea to put the home into warranty at closing. Even though the home had been given a stamp of approval by the warranty department, the warranty manager did not want to accept cognizance of the home. Even if the buyer had inspected the home and all items corrected, he wanted the construction department to maintain cognizance over the home in case the buyer discovered something new. He thought it wasn't a good idea to introduce the buyer to the warranty process immediately after the buyer closed on the home. Rather, he thought it would be best for the construction department to handle any issues discovered in the first week or two after the customer purchased the home.

Discussion. The warranty manager is an idiot. Regardless of the merits of his proposal, the implementation is seriously flawed. He implemented a new business process without discussing it with anyone. The result was chaos, confusion, and angst amongst the employees in the warranty department and in the construction department. In the middle is the customer. Due to the good graces and great nature of the construction department employees, they ensured customer needs were met. However, the warranty manager did nothing more than inject murky waters into something that was once completely clear.

Additionally, a practical problem emerged from what the warranty manager did. The process actually resulted in the homeowner not knowing to whom he should address any new issues with his home. If he found a chipped tile, he would call the construction department, who would direct him to the warranty department. Sometimes, the warranty department would direct him back to the construction. Sometimes, both warranty and construction were addressing the same issue at the same time. It was a mess.

Chapter 2: The Leader Who Loves to Make Decisions

Scenario 2: The training organization for a large, international corporation had a leader who was insecure about his leadership. To help himself feel more secure and feel like he was doing a good job, he liked to make decisions...because, for some misguided reasoning, he felt like making decisions meant that he was leading. He loved to make decisions because it made him feel like he was in charge. Also, once he made a decision, that was the end of discussion on the matter and everyone needed to fall into line. In one particular instance, he made a decision about corporate housing for resident students. Each department had cognizance over a particular block of housing, except the smallest department which "borrowed" housing from the other departments. Throughout the calendar year, the enrollment in resident training would wax and wane in a rather predictable pattern. That resulted in some departments having empty housing, while others were bursting at the seams. This problem was normally handled in an informal manner amongst the department heads to ensure all training participants were provided quality housing. The insecure leader decided to realign the housing based on a snapshot in time that poorly reflected the normal state of affairs and failed to account for the variations of student populations throughout the year. He made a decision without consulting with the department heads. Once his decision was made, I asked if there was any opportunity for discussion or reconsideration. The leader looked a bit surprised and puzzled. I explained my rationale, and he looked a little deflated at his decision. However, not to be undermined, he made it clear that his decision had been made and we would operate under the new rules he had established.

Discussion. This leader is insecure about his own leadership. How on earth he made it to a place of leadership of such a large and complex organization is confusing, but there he was. His ability to analyze data, establish a framework for decision making, and make a reasonable decision was seriously flawed. The result is that the organization is less effective and efficient. Now, as a result of his habit of making stupid decisions, the entire organization spent time and effort trying to mitigate his stupidity and work within a set of processes and procedures that were onerous and confusing.

As an interesting side note, this leader was unaware of his own shortcomings. He had a habit of setting a time for an event or meeting, then arriving several minutes or over an hour late. There were times that several hundred employees were assembled waiting for him, while he sat in his office doing nothing important. When I brought this to his attention, he seemed genuinely surprised that he was late to anything. It was eye opening for me. He was completely unaware of the weight of his poor management and leadership was having on the organization. Any accolades or accomplishments under his leadership are even greater because they were accomplished in spite of his lousy leadership.

Chapter 3: The Checklist Leader Who Only Cares About Himself

Scenario 3: A national production company has a division president who is arrogant as can be. He doesn't care about anyone but himself. He has read some books about leadership and implements some of the tools and techniques because the books say that is how to be a good leader. For example, he talks with employees and takes notes because he read somewhere that he should take notes when talking with employees. However, when he reviews his notes with the employee, it is clear that he was not listening. He already had preconceived ideas of what topics would be discussed and those preconceptions are what he wrote on his paper...not what the employee mentioned.

When he speaks during meetings, he makes eye contact. However, it appears that he is doing so because he read it in a book. It is like his mom told him to look people in the eye when speaking with them, so he is trying it out.

Discussion. This leader is a selfish idiot. I had a meeting with such a leader and was impressed when he started taking notes. However, when he reviewed his notes with me, it was clear he had not listened to anything I said. He already had in his head the points he thought I would make, so he wrote them on his paper. It became a bit more clear to me when he said that it was consistent with what others were saying. I chuckled inside and thought, "no kidding...because it is all made up in your head". He used this contrived data to show that the organization was meeting the needs of the employees.

This same leader appeared comfortable in a group setting. He seemed confident and fairly well-spoken. However, he did not value people. He only saw them for what good they could do for him. So, when it came to eye contact, it was odd and seem unnatural. It seemed like he read in a book that eye contact was a good idea for a leader, so he tried it. There was nothing natural about it, it was uncomfortable for him because he would rather talk at you than talk with you.

This type of leader is a checklist leader. He reads things in a book and develops a checklist of things that a successful leader does. He then tries to do the things on his checklist. He does them for selfish reasons...for his own gain and success...not for the betterment of the organization or the employees. This type of leader is great at making the work environment feel sad and empty and without a unified purpose.

Chapter 4: The Disappointing Jerk

Scenario 4: This leader promises to take care of subordinates, but fails to do so. He may promise many things to the employees, but does not actually do what he promises. One employee is doing a great job on a project and the boss tells her he will submit her for a promotion if the project is successfully completed. The employee completes the project and receives great praise for the results, but the boss does not submit for promotion. When confronted, he has a myriad of excuses why he will not do what he promised.

Discussion. This type of leader is a first-class jerk. When this type of leader is new to the organization, he generates lots of excitement among the employees because of his promises. However, once he starts failing to do what he says he will do, the employees begin to loath him. He is like a spider because he spins a web of excuses of why he cannot do what he promises. Many of the employees want to believe he is a good-natured person and has simply been prevented from fulfilling his promises by company executives or some newly-discovered policy. Sometimes the boss says he will make it up another way and strings the employee along, making the employee think something good is coming in a matter of time. However, the boss is really a selfish jerk who will not make the effort to keep his promises to the employees.

Chapter 5: The Boss that Cannot Speak Clearly

Scenario 5: The boss makes everyone wonder what he wants, which direction to take a project, what tasks are important, or which goals are the highest priority. He could be a very nice person, but fails to be clear when speaking or conveying what is important.

Discussion. I was in a meeting once and someone told the boss that we should do solution A. The boss said that was exactly what he wanted and was "what he was talking about". Then another employee offered solution B, that was completely different that solution A. The boss said it was precisely what he was after. Nearly everyone in the room was bewildered.   Solutions A and B were mutually exclusive so they could not both be done. As the employees began to probe for clarification, things only got worse because the boss was agreeing with everyone and everything. The boss had a serious communication problem. He was either not listening, not understanding, or not speaking clearly. Sometimes he used an odd buzz word that nobody really understood. He tried to explain, but was simply terrible at it, so everyone had a different notion of what the boss meant. Nobody knew what was important or in which direction the organization would go. It was a difficult time for the organization that never improved until that boss departed the organization. These type of people may often be well-meaning, but not fit for leadership positions.

Chapter 6: The Bully

Scenario 6: The bully is intelligent and capable of being a good leader, but actually cares more about himself and his own legacy than he cares about people. So, he uses his position in a threatening manner. He makes others feel like the possibility of adverse consequences drive their actions.

Discussion. I knew a lady who worked for a guy that would not let her sit down in his office unless she first asked for permission. On the surface, we could argue that the boss was simply instilling a proper respect for his position, not himself. But this boss was actually just a bully. He made others feel like they needed to do what he said or face adverse consequences. If his demands were not followed, the repercussions would be too great. Dissent was not allowed. Any discussion that resulted in disagreement with the boss was intensely uncomfortable until the boss got his way. These types of bosses are the cause of a miserable work environment.

Chapter 7: The Energetic Idiot

Scenario 7: There is an old adage of a Prussian general that categorized officers. One of the categories was the stupid and industrious...and those officers were classified as dangerous and should be drummed out of the army as quickly as possible. The same is true in any organization. Those who are stupid and industrious are dangerous.

Discussion. It is quite likely that you are all smiling right now because you have someone in mind. We have all worked for someone that had some "bright" idea that was actually one of the dumbest things to do. Actually, this happens to all of us at one time or another. However, this chapter is about the person that is constantly making busy work because of his inane ideas. These types of leaders generate twice the work because everyone that cares about the organization is constantly working to mitigate the effects of the stupid leader...in addition to accomplishing daily tasks.

Chapter 8: The Paralyzed Leader

Scenario 8: This leader is nice, but cannot deal with conflict in the workplace. When conflict or disagreement within the team arises, the leader cannot address it or ignores it, hoping it will go away.

Discussion. This type of leader may be very nice, but is simply paralyzed by conflict. They do not want to talk about it because it is unpleasant. They do not want to deal with it because it is too hard and involves compromise. Compromise means neither party gets everything they want, so both will be unhappy. The thought to trying to find the solution that minimizes the unhappiness of two parties seems nearly impossible to the leader and is too confusing to think about, so the leader would rather avoid it and let it work itself out on its own. However, the leader who avoids conflict is weak and allows a bad work environment to fester.

Chapter 9: The Leader Who Loves Himself

Scenario 9: I once worked with a guy who loved to talk about himself. He was a smart guy and decent leader, but when he opened his mouth, he always talked about himself. In many ways it was funny. However, when it came time to recognize an individual on the team for doing a great job, he would call the individual up, talk about himself for 10 minutes, then have the individual sit down. It made me sad for the person who was supposed to be recognized for doing great work.

Discussion. This leader is just bizarre. He may be harmless in many respects and may actually do a decent job of taking care of the organization and the people in it. However, it is very poor form to always talk about yourself.

Chapter 10: The Leader Who Loves Meetings

Scenario 10: This leader cannot sit in meeting long enough. If there were more hours in the day, this leader would have more meetings. Additionally, no meeting lasts less than 1 hour. In fact, most last 3 or 4 hours. I heard about a guy who would have the staff in marathon meetings several times a week. The staff was miserable.

Discussion. This leader has a problem managing and leading. Some leaders are more hands on than others, but marathon meetings to get to the bottom of every last detail are onerous and leave everyone exhausted. They suck the energy out of the unit and are a great demotivator.

Chapter 11: Too Busy with His Personal Life

Scenario 11: You are swamped with work, but your boss seems to have time to talk on the phone, chat with others, surf the internet, and take an extended lunch.

Discussion. This leader is out of touch with the workload in the office, which makes the work environment extremely frustrating. As I wrote in the prologue, my work is mine to accomplish and does not belong to my boss. Similarly, his work is his to accomplish and not mine to worry about. If he has plenty of time on his hands, it does not bother me. However, when there is a huge imbalance, there is a problem. If I am swamped with work, the leader should also have something to do to help coordinate efforts, streamline follow-on actions, develop future opportunities, etc. If he isn't actually working, there are a couple of possibilities. First, the employees may be doing his work, which is clearly dysfunctional. Second, the organization is quickly running out of work and will soon be disbanded. Whatever the organization produces or whatever service they provide may be obsolete, so the organization may soon be defunct.

Chapter 12: Keeping Secrets

Scenario 12: Your boss keeps you guessing about what he wants. When he asks for a report from you, he views the report and gruffs that you are off the mark. However, he fails to tell you what information he needs to see in the report.

Discussion: This leader likes to play guessing games. For some reason, he feels a sense of power or superiority if he keeps the employees in the dark, constantly guessing about what he wants. It is very true that the leader must make decisions and he needs data and information to make decisions. However, obscuring what information you need is pretty childish and absolutely counter-productive. It will dampen the performance of the organization and handicap its ability to succeed. The leader who keeps secrets is a detriment to the organization and needs to grow up.

Chapter 13: The Ungrateful Leader

Scenario 13: You boss is simply ungrateful for the effort you put into your work. He drives very hard for the team to produce results, often at the expense of the employee satisfaction and customer satisfaction, only to achieve a high number on some metric. When you produce something that is nearly impossible, he doesn't thank you, but threatens your job if it isn't better next time. Consider a residential construction company. A construction manager completes and delivers several homes to the customers much quicker than normal because the boss demands it. The boss states that the houses need to close for the company to meet their projected numbers. So, the construction manager works hard to deliver the homes and convinces several buyers to voluntarily close on the home even though they do not want to. Rather than thanking the employee for exceeding the goals, the boss reprimands the employee because the homes could be in better condition.

Discussion: This leader is awful. There is a saying that "you can have it fast or you can have it good, but you cannot have it good and fast." This adage is true in residential construction. Sometimes things can come together very quickly, but normally it takes time to build a house properly. The truth is, I am over 50 years old and have been tying my shoes for a long time. If you ask me to tie them too quickly, my shoe won't fit right and it will bother me the entire day. Building a house is much more complicated than tying a shoe, so if you ask me to build it too quickly, it won't be right.

The leader who cannot understand this simple fact is living in an alternate reality. It is possible that this leader has simply read some leadership books and latched on to the notion that "a task will take as long as you give the subordinates to complete it". In other words, if you give them two weeks to complete it, they will take two weeks. If you give them three hours to complete it, they will complete it in three hours. However, such an idea is over-simplified and rarely applicable to real world scenarios. Most professional employees strike the right balance between speed and quality of work. Many understand the customer and know when they can sacrifice quality for speed. Other times, they are aware when the customer demands better quality and is able to wait a little longer.

The leader who pushes his employees to meet near impossible deadlines on every project is not actually leading. He is only corralling a group of people and driving them to be embarrassed about where they work and what they produce.

Chapter 14: Conclusion

I hope you enjoyed reading this short book.
Maybe you can relate to some of these examples.
Maybe you can remember a time when you were
the person in this book. I can think of a couple of
times that I was the leader that I did not want to
become. The point is that we all make mistakes or
poor choices from time to time. We cannot go
back in time and make a different choice, but we
can change how we act or behave in the future.

As you read these chapters, you have probably
noted similar bosses in your past and are thankful
you survived. If we are honest, we probably
learned a great deal from these toxic leaders. We
probably learned some things we want to make
sure we never do, as well as some things we could
do better.